CW00868734

Pelagornis

Megalodon

Ranzania

EXTINCT

IN THIS SERIES BY BEN GARROD AND GABRIEL UGUETO

Hallucigenia

Dunkleosteus

Trilobite

Lisowicia

Tyrannosaurus rex

Megalodon

Thylacine

Hainan gibbon (May 2022)

ALSO BY BEN GARROD

The Chimpanzee and Me

So You Think You Know About Dinosaurs? series:

Diplodocus

Triceratops

Spinosaurus

Tyrannosaurus rex

Stegosaurus

Velociraptor

EXTINCT

MEGALODON

Ben Garrod

Illustrated by Gabriel Ugueto

ZEPHYR

An imprint of Head of Zeus

Typesetting and design
by Nicky Borowiec

Printed and bound in Serbia
by Publikum d.o.o.

Head of Zeus Ltd
5–8 Hardwick Street
London EC1R 4RG
WWW.HEADOFZEUS.COM

'We should be afraid of sharks half as much as sharks are afraid of us.'

Peter Benchley

CONTENTS

Introduction 1

† What is Extinction? 4

? Why Do Species Go Extinct? 8

  ❋ Diseases, Predation and Competition 11

  🐝 Coextinction 19

  Genetic Mixing 19

  ❋ Habitat Destruction 21

  🌡️⚠️ Climate Change 22

🕐 Timeline 24

☠ Mass Extinctions 26

🦈 The End Pliocene Mass Extinction 30

  🌡️❄️ Causes 34

  ☀️ Effects 39

🐟 Ask the Expert   48

🐟 **Megalodon**   52

    🔍 Megalodon: Discovery   58

    🦴 Megalodon: Anatomy   60

    🧩 Megalodon: Classification   71

    🐟 Megalodon: Ecology   81

Glossary   110

INTRODUCTION

For as long as there has been life on Earth, there has been extinction, and given enough time, all species will one day go extinct. Every day, it seems, we hear more and more tragic stories about more and more species being closer to extinction. There are scientists, conservationists, charities, universities, communities and even a few good governments fighting against extinction and trying to save some of our most treasured species and habitats. But, and there is a *but* to this story, extinction has its place in our world. At the right level and at the right time, it is a perfectly natural occurrence and can even help evolution in some ways.

I am a scientist. It's the very best job in the world. In my work, I look at evolution and I've been lucky enough to spend time with some of the most endangered species on our planet, as well as a few that have already gone extinct. I'm fascinated by the effects extinction has on nature, in the broader sense. But how much do we *really* know about extinction?

If we are to ever stand a chance of saving species from extinction, then first we need to understand it. What is extinction? What causes it? What happens when many species go extinct at once? I want to explore extinction as a biological process and investigate why it can sometimes be a positive thing for evolution, as well as, at times, nature's most destructive force. Let's put it under the microscope and find out everything there is to know.

When a species does go extinct, we place a dagger symbol (†) next to its name when it's listed or mentioned in a scientific manner. So, if you do see the name of a species with a little dagger after it, you'll know why. It's extinct. In this series, I have written about eight fantastic species. Starting with *Hallucigenia* (†), then *Dunkleosteus* (†) and trilobites (†), through to *Lisowicia* (†), *Tyrannosaurus rex* (†) and megalodon (†), before finishing with thylacine (†)

and lastly, the Hainan gibbon. Of these, only the Hainan gibbon does not have a dagger next to its scientific name, meaning it is the only one we still have a chance of saving from extinction.

Professor Ben Garrod

WHAT IS
EXTINCTION?

I'M OFTEN ASKED, usually by adults, because most kids already know the answer, what the appeal of dinosaurs is. Why are they so popular, so iconic, so cool? I think back to when I was young and what drew my fascination and imagination. I remember looking at (what we now know were inaccurate) illustrations of *Iguanodon*, *Diplodocus* and, of course, *Tyrannosaurus rex* and falling under their spell. But it wasn't just the dinosaurs that had me hooked. I loved huge flying pterosaurs, giant marine pliosaurs and cold, shaggy mammoths.

I loved finding ammonites and belemnites on local beaches, couldn't get enough of *Dimetrodon* and fantasised about dodos. But none of these were dinosaurs and only one thing linked them. All had disappeared from our planet. All were extinct. I think when we look into why dinosaurs fascinate kids, we are missing something. We are too easily distracted into thinking it's entirely about that amazing group which dominated the planet from the Triassic to the end of the Cretaceous period. We don't love dinosaurs because they were dinosaurs. Part of the reason we love them is because they are extinct and form part of the biggest detective story in nature. What happened to them? Where did they go? What killed them? When something goes extinct, it leaves behind a tantalising trail of questions, as well as clues, which appeal both to our scientific curiosity and our love of storytelling.

Extinction has been present since the first life on Earth popped into existence, which must mean that loads *and loads* of species have gone extinct. It's hard to get your head around how many. Scientists predict that 99 per cent of the species that have *ever* lived have gone extinct. If you're wondering how many species that might be, then if their calculations are correct, it means we have already lost an almost unbelievable five billion species from our planet.

It's nearly impossible to be certain, because many extinctions stretch back millions (or even hundreds of millions) of years and because there wasn't a scientist there with a camera or a notebook, we shall never know about many of these losses. Today, scientists believe that there may be 10–14 million different species (although some think this figure might even be as high as one trillion). Of those, only 1.2 million have been documented and recorded in a proper scientific way, meaning we don't know about 90 per cent of life on planet Earth right now.

Here's where it gets a little complicated. Extinction is natural. Even human beings will go extinct one day. It might sound sad, but that's because you're thinking from the point of view of a person. We are simply one of those 14 million or so species, remember. Usually, a species has about 10 million years or so of evolving, eating, chasing, playing, maybe doing homework, building nests or even going to the moon before it goes extinct and ends up in the history (or even prehistory) books. Some species last longer than this, some are around for less time.

Extinction helps create the rich and dazzling diversity we see across the world. It has a time and place but just because something happens naturally, it doesn't always mean it's OK to stand back and let it happen. By understanding the processes behind extinction, we have a better chance not only of knowing when to step in (or not), but also, importantly, to help us avoid getting caught up in a catastrophic mass extinction ourselves.

WHY DO SPECIES GO EXTINCT?

I REALLY LOVE spicy food. I love chilli so much that sometimes I even have it for breakfast. Weird, I know. But I also like growing chilli plants. I take the seeds from especially tasty and hot chillies, dry them and plant them in the spring, hoping for lots of plants to grow. But if I plant 20 seeds, only 10 little seedlings might appear after a few weeks. This isn't because I'm rubbish at growing chillies, but because not every seed is the same.

It's the key to the success of any species of animal, plant or any other type of organism. If every one of those chillies was exactly the same, they'd be genetic clones.

OK, there would still be differences, based on how much sun or water each gets, but at the level of their genes, their DNA would be identical. This isn't how nature usually works. Instead, every single individual is slightly different (even if they look the same) and each has a slightly different DNA *recipe*. It's this tiny variation that means species avoid going extinct every day. If something in the environment suddenly changes – making it harder to survive – that has a devastating impact on every individual.

Imagine if the temperature suddenly increases, or the levels of oxygen drop dangerously, or certain types of food that are regularly eaten disappear, then any individual within that population which, through random chance, is able to tolerate such a change stands a slightly higher chance of surviving. They're the ones that will pass on their genes and, over time, the entire population will bounce back. When there isn't enough individuality to survive such a change, or when that change is just too big to survive, then the species is likely to slip into extinction.

There are almost limitless reasons which might lead to extinction but they have one thing in common. They all focus on change. These changes can be either in the species' physical environment, such as the actual destruction of a habitat, flooding or drought. The change might be in its 'biological environment', such as the arrival of a new predator or the development of a new deadly disease. If the species does not have enough time to change or simply cannot change, it will die out and become extinct. There are a variety of general causes that can lead, directly or indirectly, to the extinction of a species or group of species.

DISEASES, PREDATION AND COMPETITION

Diseases are often linked to extinction. Practically every species alive has its own set of diseases and those which it can pick up from other species. Back in 1999, New York City became the centre of a new disease outbreak. People became sick and ended up in hospital and, at the same time, birds started dying in the city's zoo. Both humans and birds had fallen victim to West Nile virus, which is transmitted by mosquitoes. This was the first time the disease had been recorded in the USA and before long, millions of birds, from around 250 species, across the US, Mexico and Canada were either infected or dead.

In some areas, species numbers dropped rapidly by nearly 50 per cent. The risk was so great for some species, such as the critically endangered California condors, that scientists and conservationists developed vaccines to protect them from the disease and help prevent them from going extinct.

Usually, predators and prey live in some sort of balance. They have evolved side by side for hundreds of thousands, if not millions, of years. This is what we call coevolution, where the evolution of two species is closely tied together. But when a predator is suddenly introduced to an environment, the prey has no time to evolve to avoid being eaten. Once a predator is introduced into a new environment, there is often little that can be done to prevent the consequences.

Located in the middle of the Atlantic Ocean, 2,800km from South Africa and 3,200km from South America, Gough Island is among the most remote islands in the world. It is home to 22 species of seabirds and was always free from predators. However, house mice were accidentally introduced there by sailors during the 19th century and the mouse population then quickly exploded. Without pressure from their own predators, the mice evolved to become twice the size of their relatives on the mainland. And then they turned predatory.

When house mice were introduced onto the remote Gough Island in the Atlantic Ocean, they turned their attention to the seabirds that nest and raise their young there. Every year, the mice kill 1.7 million Tristan albatross chicks.

At night, they hunted nesting chicks which were not able to escape. Scientists estimate that each year, 1.7 million chicks are killed by the mice. Despite weighing around 10kg, almost a hundred times more than the mice, the Tristan albatross chicks are unable to defend themselves and are eaten alive.

So that the Tristan albatrosses are not pushed into extinction, conservationists have developed a huge programme in which poison is dropped across the island to kill the mice. Although some people don't like the thought of this, every single mouse needs to be removed if the birds are to have a chance. This will take a *lot* of time and a *lot* of money, but if we are to stop rare species from going extinct, then each situation needs to be dealt with in a different way. Sadly, we won't always love the ways we need to act to save different species.

Nature works in balance, where each environment evolves to have just the right combination of herbivores, carnivores and omnivores, predators and prey, and different types of plants, fungi and other organisms. It's like a big nature recipe and, as with any meal, too much of any one of the ingredients can completely ruin the taste. Similarly, if an environment has too much of any one thing, then problems begin and, in the worst cases, species can be driven into extinction.

This can happen even with small organisms. Harlequin ladybirds first arrived in the UK in 2004 from Japan and became one of the most common ladybirds in the country. These 8–10mm-long beetles are one of the largest of the 40 or so species of UK ladybirds. The harlequin ladybird is able to outcompete the native UK species for their aphid and greenfly prey and is able to have multiple broods of young throughout the spring, summer and autumn, giving them an extra competitive edge.

When it comes to competition, resources in ecosystems such as food and shelter might be limited and cause species to be in direct competition with one another. If a species cannot compete, it's possible it may be driven into extinction.

COEXTINCTION

Sometimes, a species has evolved alongside another species so closely that when one goes extinct, there is nothing the other can do but go extinct too. This might be a specific parasite depending on a specific host species, or maybe a particular pollinating insect needing one species of plant in order to survive. An extreme example of a coextinction is the moa and the Haast's eagle. Moa were huge flightless birds found on New Zealand, with some being as much as 3.6m in height and 230kg in weight.

The Haast's eagle was their main predator. When human settlers hunted the last moa into extinction around 600 years ago, the eagles were left with no food and they too went extinct.

GENETIC MIXING

Every organism has its own set of genetic data unique to that particular species. When you look past the physical parts and the behaviours which help define a species, you get down to the genetic blueprint, and any small tweaks can change one species to another.

Snow-capped
manakin

In the Amazon rainforest, there are three species of small, similar-looking, bright green birds called manakins. There's the snow-capped manakin, which has a white cap on its head, the opal-crowned manakin, with a shimmering opal-coloured cap, and the golden-crowned manakin. Its cap is golden, as you'd expect.

Research has shown that around 180,000 years ago, snow-capped manakins and opal-crowned manakins mated and produced a brand-new species, the golden-crowned manakin. When two species breed and produce offspring, these offspring are called hybrids. What's much rarer than individual hybrids is when you get a hybrid species. There are very few examples of hybrid species in birds. The creation of a new species like this doesn't have to pose a threat to the original two species, unless the new species starts to compete in some way, and pushes either of the original two towards extinction.

Opal-crowned
manakin

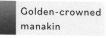

Golden-crowned
manakin

HABITAT DESTRUCTION

When we talk about this cause of extinction, we usually use the phrase 'habitat loss', but we don't lose habitats, we destroy them. Admitting this is a step in the right direction needed to protect many habitats and ecosystems around the world. The saddest thing about habitat destruction is that it means devastation, not only for individual organisms but also sometimes also for entire species.

Habitat destruction has always featured significantly as a cause of extinctions throughout the history of life on Earth. Even the world in which the subject of this book, megalodon (meg-a LO-don), evolved, habitats it needed were lost, leading to the extinction of the species. When habitat change or destruction is an influence for extinction, it might be because that habitat is completely removed, or maybe poisoned, or its temperature has changed. A whole host of changes to a habitat can bring about an extinction event.

CLIMATE CHANGE 🌡️⚠️

Some big things happen really quickly, such as a volcanic eruption or an avalanche. Others take their time, but have an impact as big, or even bigger. The biggest of these threats is climate change. It has a much larger effect than hurricanes, lightning strikes and avalanches. Any one of these natural disasters is a terrible threat. But where a hurricane might kill hundreds or thousands of animals, the effects of climate change on our planet are hard to imagine. Trillions and trillions of animals, plants and other organisms are at risk, meaning millions of species will be pushed into extinction. As our world grows warmer, our seas become more acidic and ocean levels rise, the need to act has never been greater.

It's easy to find species which have already *gone* extinct because of climate change. Animals from the bone-crunching *Dunkleosteus* (dun-kll oss-tee-us) to the ferocious *Tyrannosaurus rex* have been lost because of it.

What's even easier
is to predict which
species are *going* to
be in trouble because
of climate change, because
the answer is simple. Most of them. Unless we
act now. The only thing which is more of a threat
than climate change is not doing anything about
climate change.

People such as some politicians, celebrities and even
scientists will tell you climate change doesn't exist
or that it's natural and we don't need to act. As a young
scientist, do you listen to the evidence presented from
thousands of experts in hundreds of different reports,
or do you believe someone who wants to convince you
because they want to make money, or gain power,
or who simply doesn't understand how science,
and the processes scientists use, work? You decide.

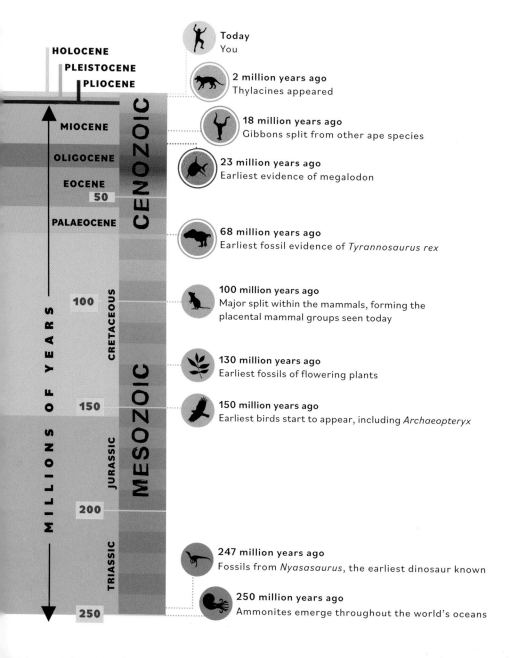

HOLOCENE
PLEISTOCENE
PLIOCENE

MIOCENE

OLIGOCENE

EOCENE
50

PALAEOCENE

CENOZOIC

MESOZOIC

CRETACEOUS

JURASSIC

TRIASSIC

100

150

200

250

MILLIONS OF YEARS

Today
You

2 million years ago
Thylacines appeared

18 million years ago
Gibbons split from other ape species

23 million years ago
Earliest evidence of megalodon

68 million years ago
Earliest fossil evidence of *Tyrannosaurus rex*

100 million years ago
Major split within the mammals, forming the placental mammal groups seen today

130 million years ago
Earliest fossils of flowering plants

150 million years ago
Earliest birds start to appear, including *Archaeopteryx*

247 million years ago
Fossils from *Nyasasaurus*, the earliest dinosaur known

250 million years ago
Ammonites emerge throughout the world's oceans

MILLIONS OF YEARS

PERMIAN

CARBONIFEROUS

300

350

DEVONIAN

PALAEOZOIC

400

SILURIAN

450

ORDOVICIAN

CAMBRIAN

500

PROTEROZOIC

ARCHEAN

300 million years ago
Lisowicia first appeared

320 million years ago
'Mammal-like reptiles', including *Dimetrodon*, evolve

340 million years ago
Earliest amphibians

382 million years ago
Earliest evidence of *Dunkleosteus*

385 million years ago
Oldest fossilised tree

400 million years ago
Earliest fossils of insects

Some of the dates for earliest fossils are estimates based on our best understanding right now. They are not always perfect and the more evidence we collect, the more certain we can be and the more accurate these dates will eventually become.

500 million years ago
Fossil evidence from *Hallucigenia*

520 million years ago
Earliest vertebrates emerged (and may have looked like small eels)

530 million years ago
Earliest fossils of trilobites

680 million years ago
Earliest ancestors of jellyfish and their relatives

2.15 billion years ago
Earliest evidence of bacteria

3 billion years ago
Earliest evidence of viruses

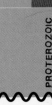

MASS
EXTINCTIONS

RIGHT NOW, somewhere in the world, something, for some reason, will be going extinct, hopefully due to natural causes. In the same way that the evolution and appearance of a species is completely natural, so too is the constant loss of species. Species come and go in a cycle, a bit like tides moving back and forth or the changing of the seasons.

Extinction is unavoidable and goes on at a fairly predictable rate wherever life exists. We call this background extinction: constant, low-level extinction which doesn't cause major problems on a wider scale – other than for the species going extinct, that is. These

Hallucigenia

'everyday extinctions' go mostly unnoticed by the majority of us. This all changes when we talk about a mass extinction.

For the purposes of my books, we are going to treat a mass extinction as the worldwide loss of around 75 per cent (or even more) of species, over a short space of 'geological' time. If you're wondering how short 'a short space of geological time' is, then let's say it has to be under three million years. This might sound a very long time, but remember Earth is around four and a half *billion* years old. By making our time frame three million years, we catch the sudden disastrous mass extinctions, such as the dinosaur-killing asteroid End Cretaceous event, as well as some of the mass extinctions which played out over hundreds of

Dunkleosteus

Trilobite

Lisowicia

thousands or even millions of years ago.

Throughout the series, as well as focusing on the five 'classic' mass extinctions, we'll be looking at the newly discovered mass extinction which claimed the mighty megalodon. The series then explores the current extinction event which is being triggered by us, before finishing on what scientists and conservationists are doing to tackle the threat of extinction and exploring what can be done.

Tyrannosaurus rex

Hainan gibbon

Thylacine

THE
END PLIOCENE
MASS EXTINCTION

WHILE NO TWO mass extinctions are exactly the same, these terrible events often have a few things in common. Usually, the more recent a mass extinction, the more we understand how and why it happened and the impact it had. An episode of extinctions becomes a *mass* extinction when it causes at least 75 per cent of life on Earth to disappear. But there is one mass extinction that doesn't play by the rules, and in fact, isn't even accepted as being a mass extinction by everyone. As we move through the geological record getting closer to where we are today, the Earth went through a series of much shorter time periods, such as the Palaeocene (PAY-LEE O-SEEN), the Eocene (E-O-SEEN) and the Oligocene (ol-i-go SEEN), which were much shorter than the previous three periods: the Triassic, Jurassic and Cretaceous.

Megalodon appeared and thrived in the Miocene (MY-O-SEEN), which came after the Oligocene, then died out in the following period, the Pliocene (PLY-O- SEEN). The species lasted for around 20 million years, which is a perfectly acceptable time when you remember that the average 'lifetime' for a species is about 10 million years.

Maybe megalodon just evolved, conquered the waters of the world and then died out, when its time was right. Seems a bit weird, though, doesn't it? Maybe even a bit fishy! When you look at the bigger picture, it becomes even more suspicious, because at the same time as the last megalodon was alive, somewhere between 3.6 million and 2.5 million years ago, something scarily familiar happened. Species started going extinct. But not everywhere.

Previous mass extinctions, like the End Ordovician some 443 million years ago, and the Late Devonian around 360 million years ago, had focused on the Earth's marine environments, mainly because there was either little or no life on the land then. But life on the land was definitely thriving a few million years ago. Then, towards the end of the Pliocene, marine ecosystems started to collapse and by the time the Earth entered a new period of time, the Pleistocene (PLI-STO SEEN), up to a third of all large marine animals, including 43 per cent of turtles and 35 per cent of seabirds, were gone.

This 'new' mass extinction was only described by scientists in 2017 and although it has increased our knowledge of palaeontology and geology, it has left us with lots of questions which remain unanswered.

CAUSES

I love reading spy novels and crime thrillers. Each book is a journey, figuring out who the arch villain is from the list of suspects, ticking them off one after the other, until there is only one possibility left. What I've never read is a book where all the suspects committed the crime, working together, all contributing in their own way. Yet this does seem to be exactly what happened with the End Pliocene mass extinction. As with the previous devastating events which killed many species and groups, there is a list of possible causes behind what happened at the end of Pliocene period.

Between 3.8 million and 2.4 million years ago, the rate of extinction seen in marine-living large animals (known as marine megafauna) was three times higher than at any other point over the last 66 million years. After the previous (and most famous) mass extinction, at the end of the Cretaceous period, and during the following 66 million years, the largest global sea level changes started occurring in the Pliocene period, around 5.3 million years ago. After the widespread formation of ice cover across the northern hemisphere, a series of cycles of sea level fluctuations followed. Tempting as it is to see a link between all that ice, huge temperature drops and the extinctions, we need to look at the clues and follow the evidence before we can be certain.

There's a very big difference between causes and coincidences, so just because a squirrel falls out of a tree on a Tuesday it doesn't mean that Tuesdays are dangerous for squirrels! But if, on *every* Tuesday, a thousand squirrels fell out of their trees, then maybe we'd need to take a closer look at what's really going on with Tuesdays.

When we look at megalodon, we know it had disappeared from the fossil record and was extinct by the end of

the Pliocene period, around 2.6 million years ago. We also know this period coincides with a time when the planet entered a phase of global cooling. To fully understand what led to the extinction of megalodon, other marine megafauna, many seabirds and various other species, we need to see whether they *were* lost because of the dropping global temperatures and, if so, what caused this period of extreme cooling? There are a number of possibilities and these may have contributed to the extinction of the megalodon in a number of ways, so let's look at them.

There is now a strip of land connecting North and South America, but between 200 million and 154 million years ago, a narrow channel of water, or 'seaway', formed, allowing equatorial warm waters to be transported all around the planet. This channel started closing around 13 million years ago and by 2.5 million years ago, the land bridge between continents had fully formed. This land strip blocked the continuous conveyor belt of water around the planet, which led to differences in salt levels between the Pacific and Atlantic oceans and affected the northward transport of warmer waters. As a result, snowfall and ice cover increased and the global climate cooled.

Another possible cause is the drastic change in the geological environments in North America and Greenland. Changes in both the Rocky Mountains and the mountains across Greenland's west coast may have cooled the climate due to disruption of the fast-flowing, narrow channels of air throughout the atmosphere, known as jet streams. This disruption of warm air currents combined with the increased height of the land caused by the growing mountain ranges led to colder conditions.

Every few years, sea surface temperatures increase, in a phenomenon called El Niño, but in the Early to Mid Pliocene, a permanent state of El Niño existed. This would have warmed the northern polar region and prevented glaciation in the northern hemisphere, helping to keep the planet warm. But around three million years ago, the permanent El Niño broke down and colder surface water led to global cooling.

Yet another factor is that during the Late Pliocene, carbon dioxide concentration in the atmosphere decreased, which may have significantly contributed to global cooling and the start of major ice cover across the northern hemisphere.

When massive stars come to the end of their lives, they 'die' in real style, ending in a truly catastrophic explosion, called a supernova. Within the body of these stars are various metals and other elements that are not found on Earth, so when we find them here, we know that they have arrived from space and are from supernova events.

One example of this is when scientists discovered levels of Iron-60, a type of radioisotope (RAY-DEE-O I-SO-tope). This is an unstable form of a chemical element that releases radiation as it breaks down and becomes more stable. Finding this extra-terrestrial element on Earth told scientists that it had originated from a supernova. But it didn't tell them when. The discovery came from the smallest of fossils, which had incorporated Iron-60 into their tiny shells, and when these microscopic fossils were dated, they were aged to around 2.7 million years ago, falling nicely within the period of the End Pliocene marine mass extinction.

With numerous possible causes behind the End Pliocene mass extinction, and so many potential factors leading to them, scientists have, so far, been unable to completely solve this recent geological mystery. However, remember that only a handful of years ago, we didn't even know there had been an extinction event. We are making progress in revealing exactly what happened and why.

EFFECTS 🔆

When the climate across the planet cooled, sea levels dropped and water became locked up as ice in polar regions, leading to the loss of important coastal and shallow-water marine habitats around the world. When we link this to the finding that a staggering 86 per cent of the Pliocene marine megafauna lived in and around such coastal areas, you can see why the loss of these important habitats was so devastating for this and other groups. It wasn't quite as simple as just changing where the coastline was,

The 1.5m-long predatory mammal *Arctodictis* discovers a large dead *Nesodon*, but a male *Phorusrhacos* has found it first and does not plan to share. These giant flightless terror birds were among the dominant land predators in South America during the Miocene.

though, as the Miocene and Pliocene periods showed a fluctuation in sea levels and therefore where the coastline lay. If species and groups were not able to adapt to this sort of almost constant change, they would have been forced into extinction.

Because it had such a large body size, megalodon required a regular supply of food to survive, but at the end of the Pliocene, we see lots of changes in the large marine mammal fossil record, as a result of climate change. Many of these whales, sea cows and giant sloths, which had been so diverse in their species and numbers at the start of the Miocene period, were lost forever, leaving megalodon with fewer types of prey to hunt and less food overall. Although there is, at the moment, no evidence to suggest climate change directly led megalodon into extinction, it does seem that this giant shark was, through the reduction and loss of its food, an indirect casualty of the global cooling at the end

Giant sloth

of this period. Additionally, it seems that for megalodon specifically, this mass extinction was made even worse because of increased competition from other new species of predators. Great white sharks and killer whales had appeared towards the end of the Pliocene and may have outcompeted the massive megalodon when it came to catching prey and conserving energy. It may have been the case that when surrounded by faster, smaller competitors, megalodon was simply too big to survive in such a rapidly changing world.

During the middle of the Miocene period megalodon numbers were at their highest. By the end of the Miocene, the global occupancy (which is the proportion of a habitat or ecosystem that is occupied) of megalodon had decreased by 36 per cent, and then by another 29 per cent during the Pliocene, before dropping into the history books.

Odobenocetops leptodon

Six million years ago, a great white shark catches an eared seal off the Mexican coast. Following close behind is a young megalodon, which was not as fast on this occasion and will go hungry.

The impact of the supernova may also have contributed to the devastation and may help explain why this mass extinction focused not only on the marine ecosystems but also mostly on the larger animals within them. As well as physically losing their coastal homes to dropping sea levels, large species would have been more susceptible to the radiation released from the supernova. Most radiation isn't able to pass very far through water, but particles called muons (MYUU-ons) are able to pass deep into the ocean's water column. Muons are passing through us all the time, but because we live on land, we have adapted not to suffer any harmful effects from the everyday levels of muons around us.

Marine animals haven't needed to adapt, so when much higher levels of radiation hit the planet, the muons did greater damage to those organisms in the water, where it would have represented a much larger radiation dose, compared to those on land. Finally, whereas larger animals are often safer than smaller animals from the effects of radiation, muons are different again. They represent a greater threat to larger organisms. Although there is no firm evidence to say the effects of the supernova radiation caused the End Pliocene mass extinction and the loss of the greatest shark ever, it certainly wouldn't have helped the chances of survival of large marine species. This mass extinction is a fascinating natural mystery still waiting to be fully solved. The event, which mainly affected mammals, seabirds, turtles and sharks, not only meant that 36 per cent of animal groups from the Pliocene would not make it into the following Pleistoceneperiod, but also created the opportunity for the global community of beautifully diverse modern marine animals we see around us today.

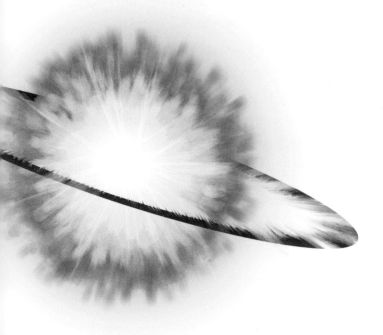

Dr Katie Strang is a palaeontologist and Secretary of The Scottish Geology Trust. She studies fish and sharks from the Early Carboniferous and uses fossil shark teeth and 330-million-year-old fossilised poop (also known as coprolites) to learn more about how these animals lived, and what the environments were like at the time.

Why should we study extinct species?

Try to picture all the different animals, plants, fungi and living things you know exist on Earth today. Do you think you could guess how many different species share our planet with us? The current estimate is at around 2 billion; but scientists don't really know for certain!

One thing scientists do know about is the different types of animals that have gone extinct during Earth's long history, including dinosaurs like *Tyrannosaurus rex*, the infamous 'big-toothed' shark, *Otodus megalodon*, and mammals such as the woolly mammoth. Before we can understand why it's important to study extinct species, we need to first understand what causes organisms to go extinct in the first place.

The fossil record tells us that there have been five big extinction events over the past 550 million years, all referred to as mass extinctions. These are events where an unusually large number of species become extinct. The most devastating occurred at the end of the Permian period around 252 million years ago, when as much as 97 per cent of marine species and 75 per cent of land animals went extinct.

It's likely that a combination of factors contributed to these events and it's important we understand what these were. Likely culprits were things like a meteor impact, or a loss of habitat brought about by changing continents like the building of the supercontinent Pangaea, or massive volcanic eruptions spewing huge amounts of carbon dioxide into the atmosphere and causing extreme warming and changes in Earth's climate.

Fast-forward to the present day and scientists are debating whether we are entering a sixth mass extinction event brought about by climate change. It is important for scientists to understand what happened during previous mass extinctions, and how different species were affected by such events. This information can allow us to better understand the future challenges we face, and help us to implement measures to avoid another mass extinction event.

MEGALODON

WE LOVE LISTS! Whether we put things in order of the tallest, biggest or oldest, we seem to like putting things in groups and in some sort of order. With that in mind, what would you say is the ultimate prehistoric predator? Maybe the planet's first superpredator, *Dunkleosteus*, with its milliseconds-fast snapping jaws? Or a sabre-toothed cat like the giant *Smilodon*, with its long, deadly canines? Maybe you've gone with most people's favourite natural killer and you're imagining *Tyrannosaurus rex*, with her bone-crushing bite? We all have our favourites and it's actually really hard to compare predators that lived underwater, like pliosaurs, ichthyosaurs and other aquatic hunters such as *Dunkleosteus*, with land-dwelling killers such as *Spinosaurus*, *Velociraptor* and, of course, *T. rex*. And with

huge flying hunters, such as
the *Quetzalcoatlus* (kwek-zal
co-at luss), to choose from,
along with a bunch of terrifying
crocodilians, mammals, birds
and other groups, it would be
hard to settle on 'the ultimate
killer'. But there is one very
strong candidate for the title of the
'ultimate prehistoric predator' and
for that, we must venture back into the
sea, between 23 million years ago and
around three million years ago.

Quetzalcoatlus

It almost wouldn't matter which part of
the world you went swimming in, because you'd
have a chance of finding one of these predators or,
more likely, one would find you. This ultimate killer was
megalodon, the largest predatory shark of all time. It
dominated every food chain in every ocean for millions of
years and would have made your chances of surviving a
prehistoric paddle slim. Megalodon was not only massive
but fast too, with what was possibly the most powerful bite
in nature ever.

When any young palaeontology enthusiast has a talk with me about megalodon, they often tell me two things. First, that there are still possibly some megalodon swimming around, deep in our oceans now. Second, that megalodon was pretty much a *very* big version of the great white sharks we see today.

OK, first things first: megalodon is gone. Extinct. Dead. No more. There really aren't any megalodons hiding in the very deepest parts of the deepest oceans. There aren't a couple just hanging out in the middle of the ocean, far away from land. You'll see why they all died out later, but for now, the main part of this message is that the biggest shark ever is extinct.

As for the 'they were really big great whites' part, that's wrong too, sadly. For many years, scientists believed megalodon was an ancient version of a great white and in many ways, it would have looked and acted the same, but fresh new scientific evidence is showing the real megalodon was a unique and terrifying killer.

Off the North American coastline, a megalodon tries its luck with a huge *Pelagornis*, a prehistoric 'toothed' bird with a wingspan measuring between 5.5 m and 6 m. Among the chaos of the *Pelagornis* and other seabirds, including extinct gannets, shearwaters, auks and a relative of the tropicbirds, a sunfish slips away unnoticed.

DISCOVERY 🔍

There's a big difference between discovering something and actually understanding what has been discovered, and the fossilised teeth of sharks are a perfect example of this. The oldest-known records of fossilised shark teeth are by a Roman naturalist and author called Pliny the Elder, almost 2,000 years ago. However, he didn't quite understand what they were and believed these strange triangular objects fell from the sky during lunar eclipses.

By the year 1300, our understanding had changed, but was still not quite right. Over the next couple of hundred years, a time known as the Renaissance, people thought fossil shark teeth were actually the preserved tongues of large snakes and dragons and had magical properties, such as being a cure for poisons. It is even said that some rich people, including royalty, often wore these 'tongue stones' to help protect themselves in case they were poisoned by their enemies.

Finally, in 1611, an Italian naturalist realised these strange triangular objects were the teeth of long-dead sharks, and in 1667, a Danish naturalist called Nicolaus Steno wrote a book called *The Head of a Shark Dissected*, which contained an image of a shark's head

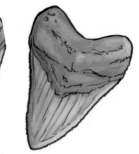

with fossilised teeth. Elsewhere in the book was another illustration of a very large tooth and this appears to be the first definite record of a megalodon tooth.

It wasn't until 1843 that this huge prehistoric shark officially got its scientific name, when the Swiss naturalist Louis Agassiz named it *Carcharodon megalodon*. There is, however, an earlier, report, from 1837, where an English palaeontologist, Edward Charlesworth, named the same animal *Carcharias megalodon*.

The scientific name has changed a few times since its discovery, but 'megalodon' is always included. It means 'big tooth' (from the Greek 'mega' meaning 'big', and 'odon' meaning 'tooth'). The big, broad teeth do look similar to those from the great white shark, which has the scientific name *Carcharodon carcharias*. Calling megalodon *Carcharodon megalodon* when it was first discovered made sense, because *Carcharodon* indicated the sharks were closely related. Later, after scientists had been able to conduct much more detailed research, megalodon was scientifically renamed, because the results showed it was not closely related to the great white after all. Species often get renamed, for lots of reasons, but you'll read more about why Meg got a name change in a bit.

ANATOMY

So megalodon was *not* just a very big great white shark. It's not accurate to say it was an ancient great white, or even that it was the ancestor for modern great whites. However, since its discovery, megalodon has at times been placed in the exact same group as great whites and, as a result, these huge ancient sharks have often appeared in films, books and illustrations looking like a massive version of a modern great white.

Of all the fossil vertebrates, ancient sharks must be one of the most difficult groups for palaeontologists to reconstruct, as they are nearly always working entirely on teeth alone. The reason for this is that usually none of the skeleton is preserved. This may sound strange, but sharks, rays and their relatives don't have skeletons like you, or in fact like any other vertebrate animals, which have an internal framework made mostly from bone. Their skeleton is made from cartilage. You may or may not have heard of it, but you definitely rely on cartilage. It's the soft, flexible material which sits at the end of some bones and helps others connect to one another. It's also the strong but flexible stuff that makes up your nose and ears. So, like your nose and ears, the skeletons of sharks are flexible, and in the same way as our noses or ears aren't preserved with our skeletons, the cartilage skeletons of sharks and their relatives also rot away and are only fossilised in the rarest of instances.

Recently, scientists have been able, we think, to piece together the few fossils that do exist from megalodon bodies, so we can finally understand not only what megalodon looked like, but also how it moved and how powerful it might have been.

Despite saying megalodon wasn't just a large great white, large modern sharks are nonetheless a good starting place from which to understand megalodon anatomy.

Basking
shark

Sand tiger
shark

Cookiecutter
shark

Winghead
shark

Megamouth
shark

Gulf
wobbegong

Great white
shark

Greenland
shark

With no skeleton, it would be easy to wonder whether megalodon was a huge hammerhead or a giant version of the weird, flat wobbegong (wob-BE-gong) maybe.

However, from its family tree and from understanding its classification, we can see megalodon was most closely related to sharks such as great whites and sand tigers, which gives us a rough outline to start from.

Megalodon is likely to have had a shorter nose, or snout, compared with the great white, and a flatter jaw, which may have looked a little squashed. The head would have been massive – over 4.5m in length (more than twice as long as an adult human) and almost 2m wide. Such an enormous head would have meant megalodon needed huge muscles along its neck and across its head to support its massive jaws and heavy teeth. Because of this, the nose would have been more curved than that of the great white, and overall, the body would have appeared stockier.

The dorsal fin, which can grow as much as 1m in height in great whites, would have been 1.6m tall (the same height as a dairy cow) and nearly 2m wide. From the top of the dorsal fin to the bottom of the belly would have measured over 4.5m and the huge tail fin was as much as

3.8m in height. Overall, and based on the best data we currently have, an adult megalodon would have been around 16m long. This isn't the same as saying this was the maximum length, just that this is the best estimate based on the fossil teeth which have been found so far. It's likely that megalodon reached 18m in length and maybe even as much as 20m long, the same as four African elephants placed nose to tail, or nearly the same as five cars in a line. Either way, it's fair to say these were the largest predatory sharks in history and were most likely the largest sharks overall, as whale sharks today can reach as much as 18m in length. Generally, they were about three times longer than modern great whites, and they weighed a *lot* more, too.

Estimating the weight of extinct animals is never easy, and there have been some intense disagreements over which was the heaviest dinosaur, but scientists have shown that it is possible that megalodon males weighed 12–33 tonnes, while the larger females reached a whopping 27–59 tonnes, which is about the weight of an adult sperm whale. The largest a great white shark can reach in terms of weight is a little over one tonne, making megalodon many, many times the size of its modern-day equivalent.

Megalodon

A few lucky discoveries have been made and some vertebrae from megalodon have been found. These have been around the size of dinner plate, helping reinforce how big this ancient predator was. There is also a possibility that part of a megalodon skull has been uncovered in Peru, complete with some teeth and some attached vertebrae. Although this hasn't been confirmed by scientists yet, if true, this would be a huge step forward in understanding the biology of the largest shark ever.

The bits of megalodon which do last and *do* fossilise are its teeth. And there are places across the planet where megalodon teeth are commonly found. The reason the

Great white
shark

teeth fossilise and the skeleton doesn't is because the
teeth are much harder, as they are coated in a mineral
called calcium phosphate, also found in our bones and
the enamel of our teeth. Megalodon teeth look like broad
triangles, with the two longest sides forming lots of very
small jagged serrations. These teeth reached up to 18cm
in length, which is almost the same length as the distance
from the elbow to the wrist in a 10-year-old human (I
bet you're looking at your arm, aren't you?). At any one
time, there were as many as 276 teeth inside the jaws of an
adult megalodon. Unlike you and me, sharks have more
than two sets of teeth – they produce teeth continually

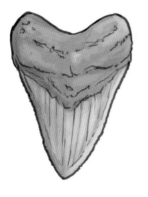 

Teeth of megalodon (left) and great white shark (right)

throughout their lives. Depending on what kind of food they eat, sharks can lose the equivalent of a complete set of teeth in a few weeks, with broken or lost teeth being replaced by new ones behind them, like some sort of dental conveyor belt. Over a lifetime, a shark might get through 40,000 teeth.

A distinguishing feature of megalodon teeth is their shape and the fine, slightly rounded serrations along each cutting edge, with 12–17 serrations per centimetre. Having big, sharp teeth was great, but they would have been useless unless they were in jaws that could open wide. In order to bite prey as large as whales, megalodon must have been able to open its mouth over 2m (and maybe as much as nearly 3.5m) wide, which is either the height of a pretty tall adult human or the same as two fairly tall humans.

One of the most impressive things about this already impressive shark was the power of its bite. Scientists are able to determine just how powerful a bite force is for living animals by using a specialised piece of equipment, where pressure sensors are inserted into a thick strap attached to a small computer. When the animal is given the strap to bite, the sensors detect how powerful the bite is. This works for some animals but not others. It's easier to train a tiger in a sanctuary or a crocodile in a zoo than it is to train the same animals in the wild, for example. It's also much more difficult to get a wild animal in the water to bite the equipment, so to test something like a sperm whale or a shark is very hard indeed.

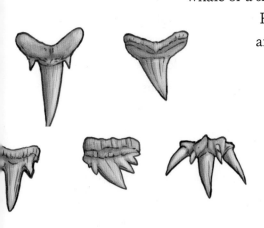

First, you need to find the animal, then tempt it to bite the equipment, and then make sure it's biting as hard as it can. You also need to make sure *you* don't get bitten in the process. It's a *lot* more difficult when you're

Teeth of (clockwise from top left): sand tiger, bigeye thresher, chain catshark, broadnose sevengill and frilled shark

working with extinct animals and again, things like extinct sharks are especially tricky. But research has been done and there are some shocking results. We measure force in a unit called newtons (or N), and as you might expect, the higher the number, the greater the bite force.

Let's start with us. An adult human has a bite force of 890N, which sounds impressive but it soon gets beaten and when we look across the animal kingdom, there are some truly powerful bites. The extinct armoured fish *Dunkleosteus*, which terrorised the seas in the Devonian period, had a rather impressive bite force of around 7,400N. This seems less remarkable when you learn the great white shark has a much greater bite force of 18,000N. When we include dinosaurs in the equation, *Tyrannosaurus rex* had a huge bite force of 50,000N. I bet you're now thinking your own jaws are weak by comparison.

When we look at the power in megalodon's jaws, though, it generates an almost unbelievable figure.

Although we will never be 100 per cent certain, because
the animals are long dead and their jaws are never
preserved, scientists have generated two numbers
for the megalodon bite force. Both are the
upper limits and focus on different parts
of the mouth – the front and the back,
which has a greater force. These studies
suggest that with its astounding bite
force of up to 93,127N measured at the
front of the mouth and maybe as much
as an astronomical 182,201N at the back
of the jaws, megalodon had the most powerful
bite force in nature ever.

CLASSIFICATION

Many species have a few different names, which depend
either on the language you speak, or where in the world
the species is found. Even the most famous member of the
shark family, the great white shark, has several identities
and is also known as the 'white shark', 'white pointer' and
even the gruesome 'white death'. These are its common

names. Every species on the planet, regardless of whether it's alive or extinct, also has a scientific, or binomial (BI NO-ME-al), name to help us identify the species, wherever you might be and whatever language you speak. Each scientific name is always written in italics and is made up of two parts.

The first part is what we call the genus (JEE-nuss) and always starts with a capital letter. The second part of the name is the species. Once a species has a scientific name, it doesn't change. But that's not *entirely* true, because sometimes, in the past, scientific names have changed. Occasionally, two scientists have described the same organism separately and given it different names when it only needed one. As our methods for understanding how we classify species, an area of science called taxonomy (tax onno-ME), improved, we needed to update some scientific names so that we can better show the relationships between organisms.

If we look at you (I'm guessing you're a 'human'), a chimpanzee and a Neanderthal, and want to see the evolutionary relationships between the three species, then the scientific names give us a big clue. The scientific name for Neanderthals is *Homo neanderthalensis* and the scientific name for chimpanzees is *Pan troglodytes*. The Neanderthals were our closest extinct relatives, and the chimpanzees are our closest living relatives, but which is actually our *closest* relative? When we look at our own scientific name, we see it is *Homo sapiens*, so because we also have '*Homo*' as the first part of our name, it shows us that we are more closely related to Neanderthals than to chimpanzees. If, for some bizarre and strange reason, we suddenly discovered from fantastic new evidence that we are actually more closely related to chimpanzees, then maybe we would have to change our own scientific name to *Pan sapiens*. The reason I'm mentioning this is because it's *exactly* what has happened with megalodon. It's one of the few species which has not only had its scientific name changed, but had it changed a few times now.

As you've read in an earlier chapter, there seems to have been confusion from the start with naming megalodon. It was officially given its scientific name (well, its first 'official' scientific name) in 1843 by a naturalist from Switzerland. This name was *Carcharodon megalodon* (car carro-don meg-a LO-don). The word '*Carcharodon*' comes from the Greek for 'sharp-toothed' and is also why a type of predatory dinosaur was named *Carcharodontosaurus* (car carro dont-O sore-us), after palaeontologists noticed how similar its teeth were to those from a great white.

However, in 1837, megalodon had already been named *Carcharias megalodon* (car carry-ass meg-a LO-don). If you know your shark science, you might recognise part of this name, which forms part of the great white name, and, more importantly, shares the first part of its name with another group of sharks alive today. The sand tiger, or ragged-tooth, sharks have *'Carcharias'* as the first part of their name, so it's pretty clear that some of the earliest studies of megalodon believed they were most closely related to either great whites or sand tigers. It quickly became accepted that megalodon was more closely related to the great white, so the name *Carcharodon megalodon* stuck. For a while. Despite being apparently unofficially renamed in 1881, it wasn't until the 1980s, nearly 140 years after it was first scientifically described,

that megalodon was renamed, this time based on a better understanding of its palaeontology and classification. The name *Carcharodon megalodon* was dropped and instead a new name, *Carcharocles megalodon* (car-carro-KLEEZ meg-a LO-don), was adopted.

This new name came into use because scientists had realised that, in fact, megalodon wasn't just a big version of a great white. The teeth looked similar but there were differences important enough to split them into separate groups, meaning also they had evolved from different ancestors. Megalodon was one of four species belonging to this new group, *Carcharocles*, which, by the time they were described, were already all extinct. It gets more confusing, though, as some scientists think there were only two (not four) species within this group. Either way, it doesn't really matter because before long, the name was ready for another update.

Now, although some scientists still use the term *Carcharocles megalodon*, most agree the newest, most up-to-date and most accurate name is *Otodus megalodon* (O-tow duss meg-a LO-don)). This classification gives megalodon a new scientific name and also tells us that the

Cretalamna
appendiculata

great white shark has not evolved from megalodon. In fact, the last ancestor they shared was well over 100 million years ago. In comparison, *you* share a common ancestor with a chimpanzee dating from five to seven million years ago.

The *Otodus* (O-tow duss) sharks get their name from the shape of their teeth. The name comes from the Ancient Greek words for 'ear' and 'tooth' because they looked (only very slightly) like sharp little ears, and although megalodon teeth definitely didn't look like ears at all, its closest relative and many of its ancestors did have distinctive, three-pointed, ear-like teeth. Megalodon's closest

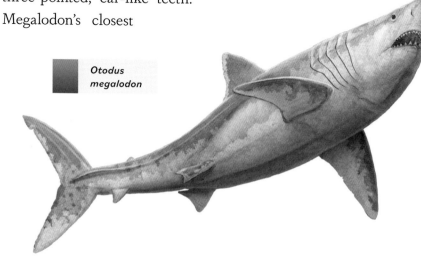

Otodus
megalodon

relative was *Otodus obliquus* (O-tow duss O-BLEEK uss). It lived 60–45 million years ago and was the largest shark around at that time, at about 9–10m in length.

Let's go slightly further back to what we now think is the direct family line for megalodon. Before *Otodus obliquus* there was *Cretalamna appendiculata* (CREE-ta lam-na a-pen-dik U-lar-ta), which gets the first part of its name from the Latin word for 'chalk' and the ancient Greek word for 'shark', because many of its fossils have been found in chalky areas. This ancestor of megalodon was smaller, at approximately 2–3m long, and lived around 105 million years ago, during the Late Cretaceous.

Understanding classification is never easy and it's a lot more difficult when we are looking at extinct organisms. When all that is left of those organisms is teeth, unravelling that classification can seem like some sort of fascinating but almost impossible piece of detective work! But we can look through the palaeontological record and see just how far back sharks go.

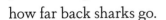

Otodus obliquus

The earliest possible evidence for the first sharks is a whopping 420 million years, before either plants or animals made it onto land. These first fossils are small scales and haven't been 100 per cent confirmed as being from sharks yet, but if they are, that means sharks have been around for almost half a billion years.

Just stop for a second and imagine all the things sharks have lived through in that huge expanse of time. It wasn't until the middle of the Devonian period, around 380 million years ago, that the first members of the group we might recognise as sharks today were alive. These fish, called *Cladoselache* (CLAY-doh sell-arch-E), had torpedo-shaped bodies, forked tails and dorsal fins and they were active hunters. They swam alongside the huge predatory *Dunkleosteus*, but technically might not have been sharks after all, and may belong to a closely related group still found today.

Sharks carried on evolving and doing well, but at the end of

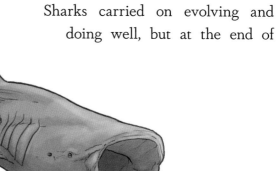

Whale shark

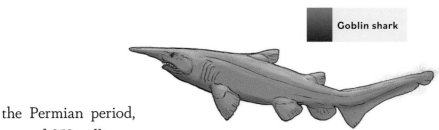

Goblin shark

the Permian period, around 252 million years ago, when the most devastating mass extinction ever, the 'Great Dying', claimed 96 per cent of life on Earth, they too were heavily affected. A few members of the shark group survived and they carried on. It wasn't until the Early Jurassic, around 195 million years ago, that the oldest-known group of those sharks still alive today appeared. These were the six-gill sharks, and many other recognisable shark groups appeared in the fossil record during the Jurassic. It was during this period that sharks evolved the ability to swim faster and developed flexible jaws able to be thrown forwards. This was a significant step for predatory sharks, as it allowed them to eat prey much larger than themselves.

Then tragedy struck again and another mass extinction affected the planet, this time at the end of the Cretaceous.

Thresher shark

Again, while most life on Earth, including many of the dinosaurs, died, some sharks survived. Most large Cretaceous sharks were lost, leaving only small, deep-water, fish-eating species. But nature hates gaps and if there is a space in the ecology of a habitat or ecosystem, it's usually not long before evolution selects an organism, or group of organisms, to fill that gap. This isn't an intentional choice or decision made by nature, evolution simply selects those organisms that stand a better chance of surviving and when they do survive, natural selection allows them thrive.

This is what happened to sharks again after the mass extinction caused by the famous asteroid. With all the large predatory marine reptiles, including mosasaurs, pliosaurs and ichthyosaurs, and all the large ancient sharks gone, there was a 'gap' in the marine ecosystems around the world for large active predators. It was evolutionary luck that there were sharks alive and able to evolve to become large predators again. A few million years after the asteroid, *Otodus obliquus*, the most likely ancestor to megalodon, appeared and dominated oceans around the world 60–40 million years ago.

Plesiosaur

ECOLOGY

Judging by where you can (hopefully) find their fossilised teeth, it seems the giant megalodon had an almost global distribution. Lots of teeth are found off the east coast of North America (around North Carolina, South Carolina and Florida), around parts of Australia and off the coast of Morocco. They are sometimes found at one or two UK locations, but the teeth from these British sites are rare and usually of poor quality.

In fact, megalodon lived in most of the world's marine habitats, except around the poles in the far north and far south, and fossils have been located on every continent except Antarctica. The most southern fossils are found off the coast of New Zealand and the most northern off Denmark.

Although they swam far and wide in the world's oceans, megalodon appears to have been specially adapted to warm tropical and subtropical locations. They could be found in the open

Squalodon

waters of the oceans,
although adults preferred to
stay closer to coastal habitats. From the concentration of
where juvenile teeth have been found, young sharks also
kept close to the shoreline, where it would have been safer
for them. Some modern species, such as bull sharks, have
their young in specific areas, near estuaries and sheltered
bays, and megalodon appeared to do the same. Scientists
have discovered megalodon nursery sites at Maryland
and Florida in North America, in Panama and around the
Canary Islands.

Sometimes, something which might seem obvious to
start with might not always be as straightforward as you
may think. Being a predator can be a bit like this because,
although it's easy to see them as being all-powerful and at
the top of the food chain, it doesn't always mean they're
safe. Foxes are predators, for example, but they are caught,
killed and eaten by other predators, like golden eagles.

When a predator is at the top of a food chain, though, and is safe from all other predators, we call it an apex predator.

It would be impossible to do, but if you took every apex predator from every habitat and environment from every stage in history, megalodon would probably be the apex predator of apex predators, due to its size, power and some specialised behavioural adaptations. Actually figuring out what it *did* eat is trickier, partly because fossils showing injuries and bite marks are rare, and also because it's unlikely much would have been left after being attacked by the biggest shark ever.

From the fossil evidence we do have, it seems that megalodon fed on a wide range of sea mammals, including now-extinct filter-feeding whales, another extinct group called the shark-toothed dolphins, large bowhead whales, sperm whales and the largest filter-feeding baleen whale group, which today includes marine giants such as blue whales and fin whales. Also on the menu was a range of seals, sea cows, turtles, fish and other sharks. Some research suggests that instead of large prey, megalodon targeted smaller whale species, 2–7m in length, and like great whites today, it's likely that megalodon fed on different sizes and types of food at different stages throughout its life.

A hungry megalodon chases a pod of 'shark-toothed' *Squalodon* dolphins through a shallow seagrass habitat, off a European coastline.

When

Megalodon were around for over 20 million years and their fossils date from as far back as approximately 23 million years ago to 3.6 million years ago, spanning the Early Miocene period to the Pliocene.

Where

Megalodon teeth have been found on every continent except Antarctica. The species had a geographical range from latitudes 55.28° N to 43.99° S, meaning they did not live in the colder polar waters.

Environment

Throughout much of Earth's history, our planet has been so different to what we experience now. At some points it was much warmer and at others, much colder. Land masses have altered due to the movement of tectonic plates far beneath the Earth's surface and supercontinents have risen and fallen over the hundreds of millions of years

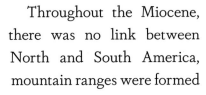

since life first appeared. But as megalodon evolved and came to dominate oceans around the world, it inhabited an environment similar to the one we know today.

As we've already discovered, at the start of the Miocene period, around 50 million years ago, the planet went through a phase of global cooling, where ice at the poles began to expand significantly. In the middle of the Miocene, about 17 million years ago, the Earth started to warm up again, and much of the planet was 4–5°C warmer than it is today. The continued movement of tectonic plates was, at the time, creating new mountain ranges around the world, including the Sierra Nevadas in North America, and the Andes in South America. Looking at the size, shape and positions of the continents, they would have been close to what we recognise today when megalodon first appeared, and by the time it went extinct, only a few areas of the planet looked different.

Throughout the Miocene, there was no link between North and South America, mountain ranges were formed

In this South American Pacific coast scene, a giant semiaquatic ground sloth, *Thalassocnus*, prepares to head out to feed, as a pair of massive *Piscogavialis jugaliperforatus* crocodilians warm up in the morning sun. The birds are *Ramphastosula ramirez* and *Spheniscus megaramphus*.

as India and Asia slowly pushed against one another, and the African and Eurasian (YOO-RAY-shun) plates did the same. This combined with falling sea levels around the world to cause the Mediterranean Sea to dry up for a while towards the end of the Miocene.

The global climate was warm, but overall, the long-term trend was that Earth was experiencing a gradual cooling. This extended from the Miocene, through the Pliocene and into the Pleistocene when a series of ice ages, and huge areas of glaciation, covered parts the planet. Towards the end of the Miocene, however, the environment across the planet became drier overall. Tropical forests across East Africa dried out, and Australia experienced less and less rainfall. Around 14 million years ago, the average temperature dropped sharply. Then, about eight million years ago, the temperature dropped even more and by this time, Antarctica had the

level of ice coverage we see today and Greenland started creating its glaciers. By the time megalodon went extinct, during the Mid Pliocene, the global average temperature was 2–3°C higher than today, sea levels were nearly 25m higher and the formation of the vast ice sheets across the northern hemisphere was well under way.

All this climate change meant there was a huge shift in the types of habitats and environments seen across the planet. It was during the Miocene that kelp forests first appeared in coastal habitats around the world and rapidly became some of the most productive ecosystems anywhere on Earth. Vast grasslands, established just before the Miocene, continued to expand, while forests shrank in size and number. This global shift in climate and the creation of new ecosystems on the land and within marine environments had a drastic impact on plants and animals.

Flora and fauna

Throughout the Miocene and into the Pliocene, many of the plant and animal species and groups were recognisable as being close to, or the same as, those we see today. For others, it was a time to establish themselves or diversify within and across environments. On land, grassland ecosystems spread across much of the planet, allowing new ranges of animals and plants to spread with them. New grassland ecosystems allowed for more grazers, such as horses, rhinoceroses and hippos.

These grasslands were also an incredibly important factor for our own group of mammals. Around that same time, apes were becoming far more diverse, with almost 200 species, our own branch of the primate family having split from a common ancestor with our cousins the chimpanzees. The first members of the group which would ultimately lead to us humans appeared in the fossil record and were walking round on two legs, around seven million years ago.

The arrival of these important grassland ecosystems is a good example of coevolution, because in the same way these habitats led to a rise in the number and diversity of group-living herbivores, a whole new range of fast predators also evolved. By the time the Miocene gave way to the Pliocene, roughly 95 per cent of modern plants existed.

It was a time of big change for flora and fauna in the marine environments. Kelp forests spread and flourished during the Miocene and into the Pliocene. The arrival of this giant brown algae supported many new species of sea life, including various invertebrates, otters, fish and even semiaquatic giant sloths which grew to as much as 3m in length and dived to feed on algae and seagrass. Other marine environments flourished too, and it was during the Miocene that marine birds reached their highest diversity ever.

Around this time, the group containing whales, dolphins and porpoises did extremely well, and while filter-feeding baleen whales are now classified into six different groups, in the Miocene, there were over 20

During the Miocene period, the number and diversity of whale, dolphin and porpoise species was much higher than it is today, and megalodon would have specialised in preying on them. Off the coast of Chile, a young megalodon approaches a group of 2m-long *Odobenocetops*, using the murky water as cover.

different groups, with many, many species within these groups. In fact, it was during the reign of megalodon that the diversity of whales and their relatives was at its highest point ever, ranging from the utterly bizarre-looking *Odobenocetops* (O-DOH-ben oss-e-tops), which resembled a 2m-long cross between a walrus and a whale, found along the coastline off Chile and Peru, to the truly magnificent giant sperm whale, *Livyatan* (liv-I-a-tan), which grew to over 17m in length, weighed just under 60 tonnes and had 40 teeth. At over 36cm long, these were the largest biting teeth, apart from tusks, ever known from any animal. Living around nine million years ago off Peru, and possibly several other locations around the globe, *Livyatan* and megalodon are likely to have come into contact, but whether they competed for food or hunted one another is uncertain.

Although megalodon may have been the super-sized megastar of the recent prehistoric marine predator community, it wasn't the only impressive shark found in our oceans during the Miocene and Pliocene periods. At a little over 12m in length, *Otodus chubutensis* (O-tow duss CHOO-but-en-sis)

may have been an ancestor or a closely related species that shared an ancestor as well as an environment with megalodon, its much larger relative. As did the broad-tooth mako, known also as the broad-tooth white shark, which at 4m in length, was a likely ancestor of the great whites we see today. Others, such as the 6m-long *Hemipristis serra* (hem-ip-riss-tiss serra), had specialised teeth which left a unique bite mark, allowing palaeontologists to discover that these ancient sharks specialised in hunting slow-swimming manatees in shallow waters.

Behaviour

If it's difficult recreating the anatomy of a giant extinct shark, when only fossil teeth are remaining, then imagine the issues with piecing together its behaviour. Behaviour doesn't fossilise, but some amazing fossils help us work out what sort of behaviours animals were performing or were capable of. But this is just another reason why science is so amazing, because very often the most difficult stuff to do is the most exciting to discover.

It's hard to interpret behaviour from fossils, but occasionally, something incredible is found. The 74-million-year-old 'Fighting Dinosaurs' discovery shows a *Velociraptor* and *Protoceratops* locked in battle, before becoming trapped and killed by sand. From the fossil, we can even see how the predator used its claws and the prey attempted to defend itself.

One fossil shows a pair of 47-million-year-old turtles, which died while mating, whereas one of the most impressive fossils showing behaviour dates back to 74 million years ago and is known as the 'Fighting Dinosaurs'. This Mongolian fossil shows a *Velociraptor* and a *Protoceratops*, an early relative of the better-known and larger *Triceratops*, locked together in an epic battle. Incredibly, the little predator has one of its famous claws dug deep into the neck of the *Protoceratops*, which itself died biting the *Velociraptor*, shattering the bones in its forelimb.

To unwrap the behaviour of the largest shark ever is tricky. The clues give a small part of the bigger picture, but what they do reveal is a fascinating glimpse into the life of the ultimate predator.

Because they are the most commonly found parts of megalodon, teeth are the place to start. For any species, teeth are useful in helping us understand what and how the animal eats and feeds. Some species, such as blue sharks and makos, have long, thin, needle-like teeth. These are perfectly adapted to spear and pierce fast-moving and often slippery fish. Other species, including nurse sharks, have dense, flattened teeth for crushing prey with hard shells, such as crabs, lobsters and shellfish. Some sharks, such as basking sharks and whale sharks, filter-feed and they have teeth so small that they are known as 'non-functional', as they are not really used to feed at all.

Then there are massive triangular teeth, thickened in the middle for extra strength, with a row of serrated cutting grooves along each edge. These broad but powerful teeth have evolved for grabbing prey and sawing through flesh, as the shark thrashes its head and moves its body. Flesh-sawing teeth like these are for dealing with mammals, and great whites and megalodon both have them. Because megalodon was so big and needed so much energy, it is likely that it preyed on whales, dolphins and their relatives, and probably on the larger species within this group.

Megalodon was a shark that would have preferred to hunt down a humpback whale rather than a much smaller and faster dolphin any day. There is evidence for this, as megalodon teeth and ancient whale bones are often found near one another, suggesting they were in the same area at the same time. Ribs from prehistoric filter-feeding whales have also been found with tooth marks that match megalodon teeth, and there is even a whale vertebra which has been split in half, possibly from a lethal bite from the giant shark.

There are fossils with whale vertebrae and megalodon teeth stuck deep inside them, hinting at a terrible frenzied attack. Sadly, almost none of these are genuine; instead, real megalodon teeth have been glued into holes in real whale fossils to look more impressive. Always look at the evidence in front of you when you're thinking of becoming a scientist. It's easy to be tricked when you want to believe something, especially when it's as cool as this.

If we agree that megalodon hunted whales and their relatives, it also seems fairly clear that these fast and often very large animals were not easy to catch, meaning megalodon would have needed to actively hunt and maybe even ambush them. To do this successfully, megalodon would have needed some specific adaptations.

One adaptation may have been its colouring. There is lots of amazing research into what colours some dinosaurs were, but we don't have the same type of fossils for extinct

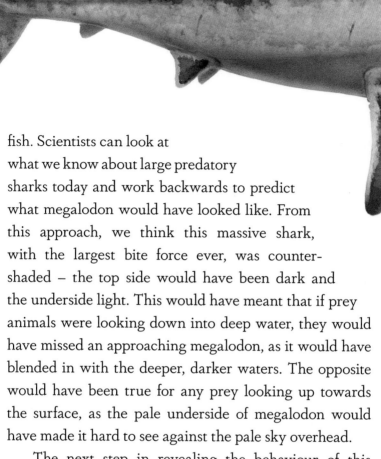

fish. Scientists can look at
what we know about large predatory
sharks today and work backwards to predict
what megalodon would have looked like. From
this approach, we think this massive shark,
with the largest bite force ever, was counter-
shaded – the top side would have been dark and
the underside light. This would have meant that if prey
animals were looking down into deep water, they would
have missed an approaching megalodon, as it would have
blended in with the deeper, darker waters. The opposite
would have been true for any prey looking up towards
the surface, as the pale underside of megalodon would
have made it hard to see against the pale sky overhead.

The next step in revealing the behaviour of this
supersized shark, after showing it had a record-breaking
bite force, preyed on sea mammals and was most likely a
mix of dark and light colours, is to see how it swam and
maybe even how fast it could move, enabling it to chase
whales. From studies into its anatomy, scientists have
estimated that megalodon had large, broad dorsal fins,

Fossil evidence from the skeletons of whales shows that megalodon hunted them by slamming into their sides, taking huge bites from their chest. This would have caused terrible damage to the whale and huge blood loss, leading to its death.

similar to those seen in great whites. Fins shaped like this allow sharks to cruise through the water for long periods without using much energy. They also allow for quick bursts of speed to ambush prey. So megalodon was able to swim for long periods of time, or across long distances, and the broad dorsal fin on the top of its body helped stabilise it, preventing it from rolling in the water when it swam fast. This perfect combination of adaptations would have allowed megalodon to cruise effortlessly along coastlines or between marine habitats in search of prey, before speeding forwards to attack. Like the smaller great whites, megalodon may also have fed on dead animals, making it both a scavenger and a hunter.

By looking at how quickly other large sea animals are able to swim and scaling up the body size of various shark species alive today, scientists have predicted that megalodon had an average swimming speed of around 18km per hour. By comparison, a great white swims at an average of about 8km per hour when cruising, but is also able to swim much more slowly at barely over 2km per hour. Unlike the great white, which often hunts by attacking from below and targeting the soft belly of its prey, it seems likely megalodon attacked differently, preferring to slam into the chest from below, as fractured prehistoric whale ribs demonstrate. With teeth able to saw through bone, megalodon may have been out to target the heart and lungs of its prey, particularly with especially large prey, as it appears from bite marks on fossil whale bones that it first disabled them by savagely biting their fins or tail to slow them down.

There is some debate about megalodon reproduction. Some scientists believe megalodon gave birth to live young, known as pups, in shallow coastal 'nurseries', where the smaller young would have been safe from larger predators.

It is also possible that the ferocious megalodons started off as predators even before they were born. Like some sharks today, they may have been cannibals inside the womb, eating their own brothers and sisters and any unformed eggs to help give them the best start in life and make them as large and strong as possible before they even had to face the big, wide world. These possible nursery sites would have given young megalodon a safe place to hide, shelter from storms and feed on other coastal prey before maturing into the largest shark the world has ever seen.

Although megalodon was the largest predatory shark ever, it wasn't the only giant predator found in the world's oceans. *Livyatan* was a species of sperm whale and although there is no direct evidence the two species encountered one another, there's a chance they would have met. What happened next remains a mystery.

GLOSSARY

Algae (al GEE)
A big group of plants that do not flower and usually live in aquatic environments. Some algae are tiny and not attached to anything. Others are big and are attached, such as seaweeds, which are the best-known types of algae.

Anatomy
The area of science which focuses on the bodily structure of animals (including humans) and other living organisms.

Apex predator
Any predator at the top of a food chain. Sometimes an apex predator will kill and eat other predators. This is also known as hyperpredation.

Baleen (bay-LEEN)
The elastic, horny material which grows instead of teeth in the upper jaw of certain whales, forming a series of thin, parallel plates. Whales with these plates are called baleen whales.

Biodiversity (BI-O DIE-vers it-EE)
The variety of plants, fungi, animals and other groups of organisms within a particular habitat or ecosystem. A healthy habitat or ecosystem will usually have higher levels of biodiversity.

Dorsal fin
The fin on the top of the body of marine animals, such as many species of fish and whales.

Ecology
The particular area of biology where the focus is on the relationship between organisms and their physical surroundings.

Ecosystem
The community of organisms (animals, plants and other major groups) and their physical environment.

El Niño
The warming of sea surface temperature that occurs every few years, typically concentrated in the central-east equatorial region of the Pacific Ocean.

Estuary
The wide part of a river at the place where it joins the sea.

Eurasia (YOO-RAY-sha)
The largest continental area on Earth, made up from the combination of Europe and Asia.

Extinct

If a species, or group of species, no longer exists, it is said to be extinct. If so few are left that they can no longer breed, even though some are alive, then the species, or group, is known as being *functionally* extinct.

Forelimb

The front pair of limbs in an animal. These can be the arms in a human, the flippers in a whale or the front pair of legs in a dog, for example.

Herbivore

An animal that has a diet based on plants.

Hybridisation

The process by which an animal, plant, etc. breeds with an individual of another species or subspecies.

Invertebrate

Any animal which does not have (and will never have) backbones, or vertebrae.

Kelp

A type of large brown seaweed. Kelp has a tough, long stalk with a broad, flat frond divided into strips. Kelp is the largest type of algae in the natural world.

Miocene (MY-O-SEEN)
A period of time which extended from about 23.03 million to 5.333 million years ago.

Natural selection
The main process that brings about evolution, where organisms which are better adapted to their environment have a better chance of surviving and therefore a better chance to produce more offspring.

Newtons
A unit for measuring force, which is when something changes the movement or motion of an object. It is the force needed to provide a mass of one kilogram with an acceleration of one metre per second per second. If an object weighs something, then it creates a force which can be measured in newtons. An apple creates about one newton, whereas the average adult human generates a little over 600N.

Northern hemisphere
The half of the Earth that is north of the equator.

Organism (or-gan IZ-mm)
Any living thing. A tree is an organism, so is a shark, and a mushroom. *You* are an organism.

Pliocene (PLY-O-SEEN)
A period of time which extended from about 5.333 million to 2.58 million years ago.

Primate
The group of mammals which includes apes, monkeys, lemurs and their relatives. Members of the group have good eyesight, five fingers, fingernails, and a few other shared features.

Tectonic (tek-ton-ik)
Relating to the structure of the Earth's crust and the processes which occur within it.

Vertebrae (vur-ter-BRAY)
Any of the backbones found in vertebrates.

Vertebrate (vur-ter-BRAYT)
Any animal within a group which has a series of backbones, or a spinal column, including mammals, birds, reptiles, amphibians and fishes.

Collect all eight titles
in the EXTINCT series

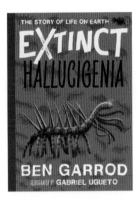

One of the oldest and most mysterious animals ever described, *Hallucigenia* was a kind of sea-living, armoured worm. But it was nothing like the worms we know today. Its body was covered in spines and frills. It had claws at the end of its legs and a mouth lined with sharp teeth.

This strange animal was one of the victims of the End Ordovician mass extinction which claimed 85 per cent of the species living in the world's oceans around 443 million years ago. What could have led to this catastrophe and what caused the appearance of huge glaciers and falling sea levels, leaving many marine ecosystems dry and unable to sustain life at a time when it had only just got started?

An armoured fish with a bite 10 times more powerful than that of a great white shark, *Dunkleosteus* could also snap its jaws five times faster than you can blink! It was one of the most iconic predators ever to rule the waves. What was it like to live in its shadow? And how did it become one of the many victims of the Late Devonian mass extinction around 375 million years ago?

Let's discover why this mass extinction only affected ocean life and why it went on for so long – some scientists believe it lasted for 25 million years. In a weird twist, we'll look at whether the evolution of trees on the land at that time was partly responsible for the loss of so many marine species, including *Dunkleosteus*.

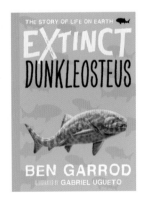

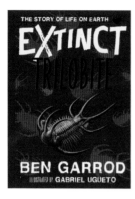

Among the first arthropods – animals with jointed legs such as insects and their relatives – trilobites were around on Earth for over 300 million years and survived the first two mass extinctions. There were once at least 20,000 species but all disappeared in the devastating End Permian mass extinction around 252 million years ago.

We'll look at why land animals were affected this time as well as those in the sea. An incredible 96 per cent of marine species went extinct and an almost equally terrible 70 per cent of life on land was wiped out in what is known as the 'Great Dying'. This was the closest we've come to losing all life on Earth and the planet was changed forever.

At a massive 9 tonnes, the elephant-sized *Lisowicia* was one of the largest animals on the planet during the Late Triassic. A kind of cross between a mammal and a reptile but not quite either, *Lisowicia* was a distant cousin of the ancient mammals – and they eventually led to our very own ancestors.

We'll discover why the End Triassic mass extinction happened, changing the global environment and making life impossible for around 75 per cent of species. And how, while this fourth mass extinction may have been devastating for most life on Earth, it gave one group of animals – dinosaurs – the chance to dominate the planet for millions of years.

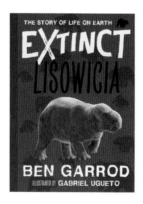

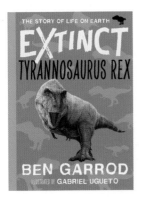

Weighing as much as three adult elephants and as long as a bus, *Tyrannosaurus rex* was one of the mightiest land predators that has ever lived. It had the most powerful bite of any dinosaur and dominated its environment. But not even the biggest dinosaurs were a match for what happened at the end of the Cretaceous, about 66 million years ago.

What happened when an asteroid travelling at almost 40,000km/h crashed into Earth? Creating a shockwave that literally shook the world, its impact threw millions of tonnes of red-hot ash and dust into the atmosphere, blocking out the sun and destroying 75 per cent of life on Earth. Any living thing bigger than a fox was gone and this fifth global mass extinction meant the end of the dinosaurs as we knew them.

The thylacine, also known as the Tasmanian tiger, is one of a long list of species, ranging from sabre-toothed cats to the dodo, that have been wiped out by humans. The last wild thylacine was shot in 1930 and the last captive thylacine alive died in a zoo in 1936.

We'll explore the mass extinction we are now entering and how we, as a species, have the power to wipe out other species – something no other single species is able to do. Who are the winners and losers and why might it take over seven million years to restore mammal diversity on Earth to what it was before humans arrived?

One of the most endangered animals on our planet, the Hainan gibbon is also one of our closest living relatives. Family groups of these little primates live in the trees on an island off the south coast of China and they feed on leaves and fruit.

But the gibbons are now in serious trouble because of the effects of human population increase around the world and habitat destruction. Without action, this animal might soon be extinct and need a dagger after its name. What can we all do to help stop some of our most interesting, iconic and important species from going extinct?

BEN GARROD is Professor of Evolutionary Biology and Science Engagement at the University of East Anglia. Ben has lived and worked all around the world, alongside chimpanzees in Africa, polar bears in the Arctic and giant dinosaur fossils in South America. He is currently based in the West Country. He broadcasts regularly on TV and radio and is a trustee and ambassador of a number of key conservation organisations. His debut six-book series *So You Think You Know About... Dinosaurs?* and *The Chimpanzee and Me* are also published by Zephyr.

GABRIEL UGUETO is a scientific illustrator, palaeoartist and herpetologist based in Florida. For several years, he was an independent herpetologist researcher and authored papers on new species of neotropical lizards and various taxonomic revisions. As an illustrator, his work reflects the latest scientific hypotheses about the external appearance and the behaviour of the animals, both extinct and extant, that he reconstructs. His illustrations have appeared in books, journals, magazines, museum exhibitions and television documentaries.

Zephyr is an imprint of Head of Zeus.
At Zephyr we are proud to publish books
you can read and re-read time and time
again because they tell a brilliant story
and because they entertain you.

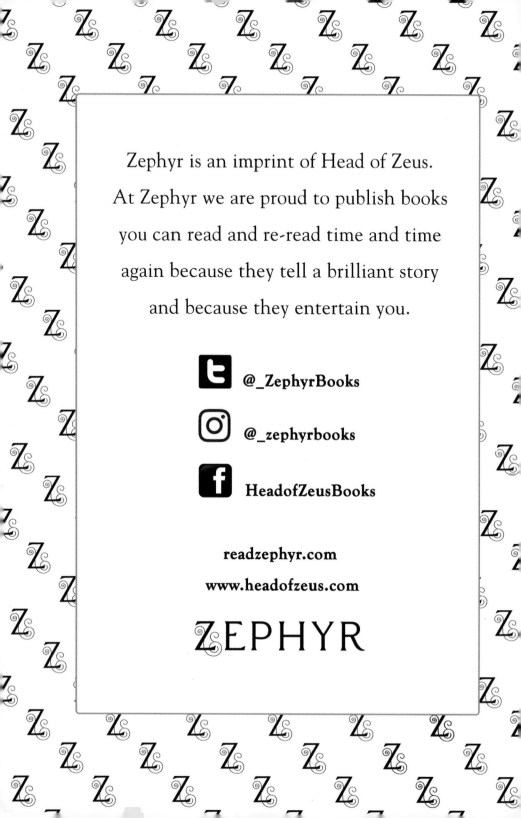 @_ZephyrBooks

@_zephyrbooks

HeadofZeusBooks

readzephyr.com

www.headofzeus.com

ZEPHYR

Pelagornis

Leptophoca proxima